Carl White

Bells Beneath the Sea
Photographs of the Suffolk Heritage Coast

Introduction by Andrew Hurst

First published 2009
Copyright © Carl White, 2009
The moral right of the author in this work has been asserted

All rights reserved. No parts of this publication may be reproduced,
stored in a retrieval system, or transmitted, in any form or by
any means electronic, mechanical, photocopying, recording
or otherwise, without prior permission of Old Pond Publishing.

ISBN 978-1-906853-15-0

A catalogue record for this book is available from the British Library

Published by

Old Pond Publishing Ltd
Dencora Business Centre
36 White House Road
Ipswich IP1 5LT United Kingdom

www.oldpond.com

Cover design and book layout by Carl White and Liz Whatling
Printed and bound in Malta by Gutenberg Press

For my parents Margaret and Philip

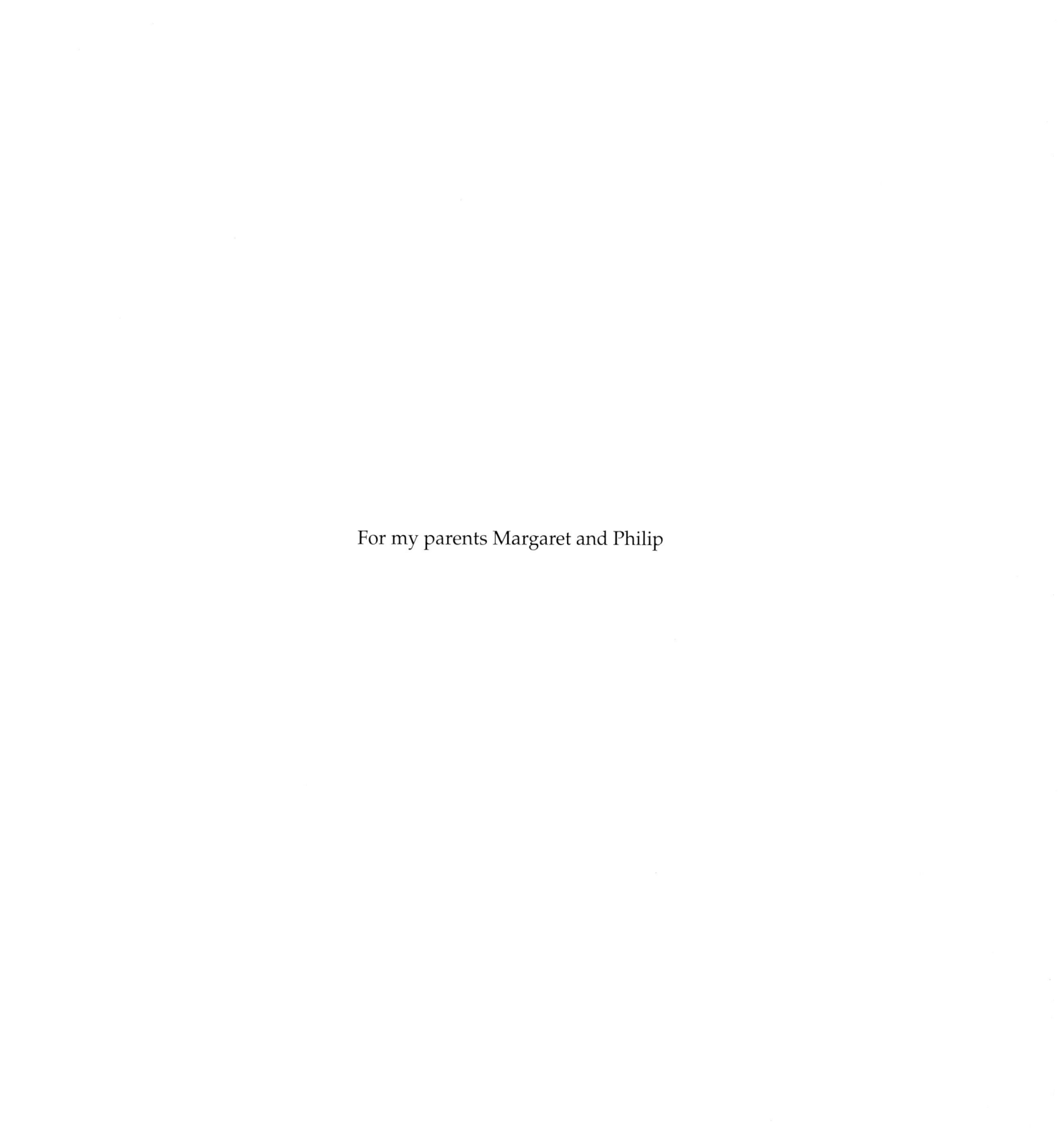

Introduction by Andrew Hurst

All counties are old; but Suffolk gives us age that resonates. To reach the coast one drives for some time, or takes a snaking train with changes to branch lines, passing through rich wool country with its prosperous Cathedral churches and its Constable pasture and woodlands. At last, after the confines of the car or carriage, there comes the long walk over pebbles that steal your stride and make you work – really work, if laden with kit or children – before you come over two or three heavy drops to stand on the shore and watch the big waves crashing in and hiss away in retreat over the stones. Here is the big sky, the vast sea, the buffeting wind and mile after mile of shore – bending, curving, rounding, but going on and on to the unseen horizon.

This is no sun-spot or fairground attraction; there are no warm blue sea or crystal wave – yet for many it is the best coast that we know in all seasons, the most compelling, arresting and awe-inspiring. It dwarfs us, soaks us and chills us, and is hard to turn away from. But why so? The answer, perhaps, is because it speaks to us, tells us gently or ferociously, but nonetheless beautifully – unlike cancer or random cruel events – that we are small, insignificant in the end, and only here on terms that are not our own, but part of something so big which we cannot really comprehend. And this sense acknowledged, realised so gently, can leave us happier, cleaner, reappraised or refreshed, in ways a hot-sand beach never could.

Carl takes his title from the town of Dunwich – now long disappeared into the sea and swallowed up in mud and waves, criss-crossed only by fishermen and sailing boats. Commerce, domesticity and faith – the town has boasted, at various times, ten churches, two monasteries and three chapels – all fallen from the cliff and taken, or re-claimed, by the sea. It is said that on certain tides the fishermen can hear the bells still ringing, deep beneath the waves.

That is an arresting thought, and leads the contemplative figure on the shore, if he or she is so minded, to think on and on of all of those mind-spinning thoughts of mortality, endeavour, purpose and futility. For those with a faith the fate of the Dunwich churches might confirm or unsettle the belief that the believer wishes to believe – that there is a God, all of this is the work of God, and that God takes us back in the end; or, for the atheist, that we are no more than earth slipping into the sea, insignificant and ultimately pointless – and godless.

We can look at these pictures and be forgiven an initial sense of despair – all those little huts clinging to cliff and beach, vast looming Sizewell, blasted trees and rotting boats.

But look again, and closer, and we see the sense of this coast and why it draws us back, keeps us, makes us reluctant to leave. In many the wind and the waves are tangible – we can step in and feel the stones beneath our feet or running through our hands, the seaweed slipping through our fingers; we hear the thump of the wave on the shore and feel the sting of spray on wind-blown cheeks; we taste the smell of the sea and feel the smooth pebble spinning from the hand to be engulfed in a wave, or feel the cold lap of water on shuddering skin. We recall the rejoicing, the laughter, the calling and shouting out, or the quiet looking and wonderment.

In *Reeds at Eastbridge* Carl introduces us early to a recurrent theme – of our lives bent by nature: here the reeds make a graceful curl – a wave perhaps? Later we shall see *Reeds at Reydon* – the cut reed drying and harvested for our use. Then we have, plainly, the conceit of all our defences – from the ruined *Martello Tower, Bawdsey* from conflicts generations ago to one still close, embodied in those squat pillboxes, defiant little concrete defenders never, in the end, tested by a mortal enemy but undone by the sea. At Bawdsey the pill box appears still intact and is busy walking towards the sea – not so much beaten but surrendering. This coast has always been threatened – before Napoleon and Hitler there were Vikings and pirates.

Carl takes us to the farming hinterland and juxtaposes *Farmland at Iken* with *Dead Tree, Iken Cliff*. We have the times changing – the arable land of wheat fields are complemented by *Turf Farm, Sudbourne*, the formerly haphazard grazing livestock is over-reached by the utility *Pig Farm, Iken* with those little dome shelters for the pigs. We have *Snape Maltings*, its original purpose transposed into a now long-established concert hall and shopping outlet.

But we have something more: most of what we make as humans seems easily to be ugly or scarring, such as *Kessingland* caravans – but give nature its influence and even a grave insult to the landscape can be redeemed: in *Field at Iken* the polythene sheeting laid to force the crop takes on a river-sheen in a shaft of sun through black cloud, and so the field is redeemed, shining like moonlit water. Do we then need nature to give our human effort true beauty? (Look again at the houses in *Westleton*.) The closest we can come is in our churches which, after all, take as their inspiration something not of human worth – and even here Carl has caught a retreat – opposite *Thorpeness Golf Course, Covehithe Church* is shrinking behind its grander ruin but its faith still flickers on. And when we see our own attempts at lighting on a grand scale – *Sizewell Nuclear Power Station* lit up at night – we know we cannot save ourselves like nature can.

When we build we often build ugly – *Lowestoft Promenade* or the *Beach Huts, Sizewell*. But we can build better, like the curious toy-like Thorpeness (but its origins Roman) with its pleasure Mere, and we can build and build well – in graceful Aldeburgh and neat Southwold. These two towns seem strong and safe behind their beaches. Carl's pictures of Southwold from within are all that the confident, safe, dry little town should be: snug, secure, protective and safe. But from the sea there is the other view: we see it threatened, tiny, vulnerable, gathered around and under its lighthouse for protection. Again and again the sea and the wind come in to take from us all that we do and put us in our place, sometimes with breathtaking glory and for the sheer wondrousness of it. In *Hailstorm from Minsmere Cliff* the sea and the storm combine into such an extraordinary spectacular that it is impossible to understand what is happening – except that it is fantastic, fantastical, and must have provoked great shouts of inarticulate joy. It is an amazing picture. The sea, in solo performance, graces the shore with fantails of surf in *Surf from Dunwich Cliff*, great swirling patterns moving and changing by the moment, captured for a second in the picture.

This is a coast that knows about death, its imminence and its passing – we see the *Grave, Dunwich Cliff* that is almost over the edge and *Covehithe Cliffs* where the fissure in the ground tells us that the tree is doomed. Nothing is spared in the end. We know too from the frail little fishing boats and the tumbledown, utility huts that the first thing the fisherman has is respect for the sea, and that everything is done on its terms, and that even then there are no guarantees. In *Sunken Boat, Iken Cliff* the boat is more a skeleton, atrophying in the river where once it would have ridden the tide with pomp and purpose.

Life and death passing, time passing: Turner was here in the early nineteenth century, creating his big seascapes and the darkening skies that Carl has captured again through his contemporary medium 160-odd years later. Turner found something haunting at Dunwich, painting All Saints Church on the cliff, the storm clouds a malevolent blue boiling up from the very surface of the sea as brave, straining figures launch a boat and themselves into peril. Turner's All Saints is gone: the east end of the church fell into the sea in 1904 and the tower toppled onto the beach in 1919. He visited Orfordness and painted another storm and a swamping sea and a shipwreck right under the safety of the lighthouse, and so Turner captured our limitations, too.

Turner's painting is one record in a centuries' long history of prosperity, gain, diminution and oblivion. Dunwich was a Roman settlement, as were Covehithe and Thorpeness. It always was an important market town. The coast was firmly Roman: remains of Roman salt-pans have been found at Snape, Iken and Blythburgh. Dunwich is there in the Domesday Book and is recorded already as losing land; by the seventh century there is evidence that, with Burgh and Iken, it was an important monastic site, and by the reign of Henry II it was a gated city enclosed by a ditch and banks and with four gates to guard it. Dunwich sent ships to war and took sides in civil conflict, but by 1832 had so declined that in that year it lost its Member of Parliament.

From history we go to Sizewell, from the *View Parking, Minsmere* and then travel down to *Felixstowe Docks,* and remember that our world depends on electricity and trade, on each other and strangers far apart. Suffolk has always given us power and commerce and so nourishes us and sustains us, whilst all the while telling us the truth about ourselves and where we stand in all of this. In *Furthest Point East, Lowestoft,* the figure points to the horizon and there, the subject of the conversation or not, is a ship far away.

This coast has inspired countless artists: on a grand scale there is the music of Britten; there is the tangible manifestation in Maggie Hambling's Scallop that the children clamber upon at Aldeburgh beach; there are, no doubt, countless writers, poets, potters and painters from the quiet and private amateur to Turner's flowing canvasses or John Nash's exquisite line drawings of the summer sea plants that flower in the shingle on Aldeburgh beach. And in Carl's pictures – no easy medium whatever the cynics might say – we have the work of a number of years, over the years, capturing yet another sense of this shifting yet unchanging place. The photographer has an intimacy with the landscape and the detail; there is contemplation about these quiet places, such as Eastbridge where the fine and graceful curves of the gate's structure contrasts with the tumble down and improvisation of *Gates and Fences, Eastbridge.* At *Leiston Abbey* the surrounding fields emphasise the forced and natural quiet on a place that was built for structured contemplation.

Perhaps *Furthest Point East, Lowestoft* tells us that our possibilities are endless and our horizons infinite. But one more picture tells us the particular truth that this coast gives us. Perhaps it is that truth that the tiny figure on the shore at *Thorpe Ness* is contemplating as he or she regards the waves – that sense that we all must know when we look at the sea and shout above the wind and waves, that whatever way we live, work, love, innovate, worship, defend or fight, our place here is on nature's terms, and we can be glad for it.

Andrew Hurst
May, 2009

Dunwich Beach

Thorpeness

House, Walberswick Quay

The River Butley, Chillesford

Reeds at Eastbridge

Martello Tower, Bawdsey

Sizewell Beach

Aldeburgh

Beach Huts, Walberswick

Dead Tree, Iken Cliff

Farmland at Iken

Beach Huts, Sizewell

Hailstorm from Minsmere Cliff

Grave, Dunwich Cliff

Covehithe Cliffs

The River Alde and Iken Cliff

Oak Tree, Dunwich Forest

Sunken Boat, Iken Cliff

Blythburgh

Gateway, Eastbridge

Thorpeness Beach

Aldringham

Gates and Fences, Eastbridge

Kessingland

Field at Iken

Thorpeness Golf Course

Covehithe Church

Westleton

Snape Bridge

Fishing Huts, Southwold Quay

Aldeburgh

Westleton Heath

Leiston Abbey

Pig Farm, Iken

Pastureland, Westleton

Fishing Nets, Sizewell

Southwold

Landguard Fort, Felixstowe

Orford Castle

Aldeburgh Bay from Thorpeness

Aldeburgh Beach

Woodbridge

Barn near Boyton

Disused Windmill, Dunwich River

Greyfriars Monastery, Dunwich

Dingle Wood

Southwold

The River Blyth at Walberswick

Reeds at Reydon

Iken Cliff

Sunset at Iken

Sizewell Nuclear Power Station

Orford Ness

Walberswick Quay

The Mere, Thorpeness

Sailing Barge, Snape Bridge

Sailing Barge, Walberswick Beach

Coastguard Cottages, Sizewell

Footpath at Iken Cliff

Pillbox on Thorpeness Cliff

The Same Pillbox

Walberswick Beach

Dunwich Beach

Iken Cliff

Minsmere from Eastbridge Sluice

Lowestoft Promenade

Aldeburgh Promenade

Tree near Boyton

Bawdsey

Bawdsey Ferry

Snape Church

Felixstowe Docks

St James' Green, Southwold

Groynes, Southwold

Alde Estuary at Iken Cliff

Hurricane Damage, Tunstall Forest

Turf Farm, Sudbourne

Dead Oak Branch, Covehithe

Eastbridge Sluice

Southwold Beach

Low Tide, Iken Cliff

Fishing Gear, Sizewell

Snow Squall, Aldeburgh

Ruined Chapel, Eastbridge

Birches, Thorpeness

Crashing Wave, Aldeburgh

Dunes, Walberswick

Ramsholt Church

Corporation Marshes

Boardwalk, Sizewell

Shingle Street

Surf from Dunwich Cliff

Tidemill, Woodbridge

Pylons, Sizewell

View Parking, Minsmere

Southwold

Cows at Eastbridge

Thorpeness Beach

Aldeburgh from Thorpeness

Sudbourne Marshes

Snape Maltings

Seagulls, Southwold Quay

The River Alde, Slaughden

Thorpe Ness

Furthest Point East, Lowestoft

Photographer's Afterword

All the photographs in this book were taken on black and white film and therefore exist as prints on traditional silver photographic paper. Over my career, photographic technology and materials have changed enormously, and, despite the discontinuation of some fine films and papers, I am very happy with the quality of materials that are available today. However, today's materials do not seem to be quite as forgiving, and to get the best results requires following instructions carefully.

I generally only photograph when the light is right, as I don't like to force the materials outside their optimum performance range, and capturing the atmosphere correctly always produces a more evocative photograph. This means I have to spend a lot of time in the field either waiting patiently or making notes as to when I think the conditions might be right. A bit of luck is never refused, though, and sometimes I get a good photograph straight away, but I get much luckier the more time I put in. *Hailstorm from Minsmere Cliff* was taken at the end of February, which is normally when this sort of weather comes along, but I did sit in my car for five days waiting for one to pass directly overhead. The seagulls taking off from the sea was pure luck!

The end result of my type of photography is the 'fine print'. This not only means working with high-quality equipment and materials but a level of craft to use them effectively – it is impossible to make a fine print from a bad negative.

Securing a good negative requires precision, and is essential to making the printing much easier and on the best possible material. However the perfect negative is not simply a matter of a correct exposure; the negative must contain all the relevant information at its correct exposure. The process in achieving this is called visualisation.

Visualisation involves seeing the finished print in the mind before the photograph is taken; it is when all decisions on tone, contrast, light and dark are made – the values of a print. It is at this point that the photographer is describing what he sees and, more importantly, feels about the subject. Ansel Adams' motto when visualising a scene was, 'What do I see, how do I see it, how do I execute the photograph?' Once visualisation is complete the photographer then works backwards towards the negative, applying photographic tools available, the most important considerations being filtration on the lens and development of the film.

Photographer Barry Thornton asked me if I saw in black and white. I replied that (of course!) I didn't but that I knew what he meant. I said that whilst I see in colour I translate it into black and white. In fact, understanding colour is absolutely fundamental to black and white photography; for example, a straight photograph, on normal panchromatic black and white film, of rich green foliage under a deep blue sky, would render too dark and too light respectively. The colour must be translated into tones of grey that reflect our emotions.

This is why craft and precision are essential if the photograph is to be the 'equivalent' of how I saw and felt about the subject. Once the calculations are made I make the exposures and develop the film according to the level of contrast in the scene, a process known as the Zone System. Again, developing the film is a precise action; temperature and agitation are crucial in controlling contrast and density. Film developing must be made with accurate consistency and according to manufacturers' instructions. This way any problems of poor negatives can be looked for in other places, such as incorrect exposure or a mechanical camera fault. I will not be disturbed when developing films … sheet films require total darkness!

Printing is best when it is the least complicated, on the best grade of paper and with the minimum of dodging and burning. Too much jumping around the enlarger with sheets of bendy card and odd shapes on the end of long wires usually means the negative is not good enough. Consistency is again absolutely necessary. I make up dish solutions accurately and maintain temperatures throughout the session. Personal print value preferences can come into play and methods can be changed accordingly, but the controls must be understood. I like to print on a warm-tone paper because I prefer the colour, but if the print is overdeveloped or treated incorrectly in the post-fix toner, the colour will be altered. I begin a print by making many test strips, normally with the lowest grade paper or filter I think appropriate. The first foot on the ladder is exposure, finding the correct tone for the highlight areas; paper grade or filtration is then used to control the dark areas. Careful testing saves time and money – efficiency makes good photographers, not boxes and boxes of film and paper.

Although making a print is a simple combination of paper grade and exposure, getting the right combination requires careful attention to all the values of a print. These values, mainly tonality, can also be controlled by how the print is treated in the developer, and if the print is treated in a post-fix toner, and how the print is washed.

There is a big difference between a good print and a fine print. This can often be only very subtle, but the difference is profound, and although there are extensive technical attributes to consider, a fine print has just the right feel which is quite indescribable. While I was working as a young photographer in America I saw a big exhibition of Ansel Adams and I remember standing before a very large print of *Half Dome, Blowing Snow, Yosemite National Park, 1955* shaking my head in breathless disbelief saying '... how …?'

As far as composition is concerned, I find it difficult to explain exactly why I am moved to take a photograph. Unless I am actually commissioned to take a photograph, I am happy to let the subconscious flow; it often works best. In an interview with David Sylvester in 1966, painter Francis Bacon said 'If anything ever does work in my case, it works from that moment when consciously I don't know what I'm doing'… and Fay Godwin's photograph *Large White Cloud near Bilsington, Kent 1981* was taken when she was supposed to be photographing a monument. Visual stimulation, and the massive memory bank of images and experiences in the subconscious, trigger the impulse to photograph.

For me there are of course quite definite interests and influences that affect my work: nature, geomorphology, weather, the heroic achievements of Ansel Adams and Fay Godwin and the creative photography culture, books by John Muir, paintings by Turner, the movies, cricket, and fish and chips. But to understand how making a satisfying photograph grips my imagination is inexplicable. One of my favourite photographs in this book is *Barn near Boyton*. It is a perfect negative, and prints like a dream, but it satisfies me far more than just its technical qualities. We all have, for example, our favourite view or piece of music, but apart from descriptions of its obvious physical qualities, we find it impossible to realise the deeper emotional relationship that we know exists but can't quite make tangible. I do know that this grip is a result of combining interests and influences – a great sphere of conscious and unconscious, serious and trivial experiences, all digested into producing the photograph.

Carl White
Cambridge, 2009

Working Information

Title	Format	Film	Lens	Filter	Exp.	Dev.
1. Dunwich Beach 2001	6x6	Pan F	80mm	Red	N+1	N-1
2. Thorpeness 2002	6x6	Pan F	80mm	Y/G	N+1	N-1
3. House, Walberswick Quay 2003	6x6	Pan F	50mm	Y/G	N	N
4. The River Butley, Chillesford 2003	6x6	Delta 100	50mm	Y/G	N+1	N-1
5. Reeds at Eastbridge 1998	6x6	Delta 100	50mm	Red	N	N
6. Martello Tower, Bawdsey 2001	6x6	Delta 100	50mm	Y/G	N	N
7. Sizewell Beach 2004	6x9	Delta 100	90mm	O	N+1	N-1
8. Aldeburgh 2001	6x6	Pan F	80mm	Y/G	N	N
9. Beach Huts, Walberswick 2004	6x9	Pan F	90mm	O	N	N
10. Dead Tree, Iken Cliff 2000	6x6	Pan F	80mm	Red	N+1	N-1
11. Farmland at Iken 2005	6x9	Delta 100	90mm	O	N	N
12. Beach Huts, Sizewell 1995	10x8	FP4	300mm	O	N	N
13. Hailstorm from Minsmere Cliff 2003	6x6	Delta 100	50mm	Y/G	N	N+1
14. Grave, Dunwich Cliff 2004	6x6	Agfa 100	80mm	Y/G	N	N
15. Covehithe Cliffs 1998	10x8	HP5	165mm	Y/G	N+1	N-1
16. The River Alde and Iken Cliff 2005	6x9	Delta 100	90mm	O	N	N
17. Oak Tree, Dunwich Forest 1998	10x8	HP5	300mm	O	N	N
18. Sunken Boat, Iken Cliff 2006	6x9	Delta 100	90mm	O	N+1	N-1
19. Blythburgh 2001	6x6	Pan F	50mm	Y/G	N+1	N-1
20. Gateway, Eastbridge 2000	6x6	Agfa 100	50mm	Y/G	N	N
21. Thorpeness Beach 2005	6x9	Delta 100	90mm	O	N	N
22. Aldringham 2005	6x9	Delta 100	90mm	O	N	N
23. Gates and Fences, Eastbridge 1998	10x8	HP5	300mm	Y/G	N+1	N-1
24. Kessingland 2000	6x6	Agfa 100	50mm	Y/G	N	N
25. Field at Iken 1999	6x6	Agfa 100	50mm	Y/G Grad	N	N
26. Thorpeness Golf Course 2001	6x6	Delta 100	80mm	Y/G	N+1	N-1
27. Covehithe Church 1998	10x8	HP5	165mm	Y/G	N+1	N-1
28. Westleton 2006	6x9	Delta 100	90mm	O	N	N
29. Snape Bridge 1998	10x8	FP4	300mm	O	N	N
30. Fishing Huts, Southwold Quay 1997	10x8	FP4	300mm	O	N	N
31. Aldeburgh 2005	6x9	Delta 100	90mm	O	N+1	N-1
32. Westleton Heath 2002	6x6	Agfa 100	80mm	Y/G	N	N
33. Leiston Abbey 1997	10x8	HP5	165mm	Y/G	N	N
34. Pig Farm, Iken 1999	6x6	Agfa 100	50mm	Y/G	N	N
35. Pastureland, Westleton 2000	6x6	Pan F	80mm	Y/G	N+1	N-1
36. Fishing Nets, Sizewell 2001	6x6	Delta 100	50mm	Y/G	N	N
37. Southwold 2006	6x9	Delta 100	90mm	O	N+1	N-1
38. Landguard Fort, Felixstowe 2003	6x9	Delta 100	90mm	O	N+1	N-1
39. Orford Castle 2003	6x6	Delta 100	50mm	Y/G	N	N
40. Aldeburgh Bay from Thorpeness 2004	6x6	Delta 100	150mm	Y/G	N+1	N-1
41. Aldeburgh Beach 1997	10x8	FP4	300mm	O	N+1	N-1
42. Woodbridge 2000	6x6	Agfa 100	50mm	Y/G	N	N
43. Barn near Boyton 2006	6x9	Pan F	90mm	O	N	N
44. Disused Windmill, Dunwich River 2008	6x9	Delta 100	90mm	O	N	N
45. Greyfriars Monastery, Dunwich 1997	10x8	FP4	300mm	O	N+1	N-1
46. Dingle Wood 2000	6x6	Pan F	80mm	Y/G	N	N
47. Southwold 2002	6x6	Delta 100	50mm	Y/G Grad	N+1	N-1
48. The River Blyth at Walberswick 1998	6x6	Pan F	50mm	Y/G	N+1	N-1
49. Reeds at Reydon 1997	0x8	FP4	165mm	Y/G	N+1	N-1
50. Iken Cliff 1988	6x6	Pan F	50mm	Red	N+1	N-1
51. Sunset at Iken 1989	6x6	Pan F	50mm	Red Grad	N+1	N-1
52. Sizewell Nuclear Power Station 2003	6x6	Delta 100	50mm	Y/G	N	N
53. Orford Ness 2006	6x9	Delta 100	90mm	O	N	N
54. Walberswick Quay 1987	6x6	Agfa 100	150mm	Red	N+1	N-1

#	Title	Format	Film	Lens	Filter	Exp	Dev
55.	The Mere, Thorpeness 2005	6x9	Delta 100	90mm	O	N+1	N-1
56.	Sailing Barge, Snape Bridge 1988	6x6	Pan F	80mm	Y/G	N	N
57.	Sailing Barge, Walberswick Beach 1998	10x8	HP5	300mm	O	N	N
58.	Coastguard Cottages, Sizewell 1983	35mm	Pan F	24mm	Red	N	N
59.	Footpath at Iken Cliff 1994	6x6	Pan F	50mm	Y/G	N+1	N-1
60.	Pillbox on Thorpeness Cliff 2005	6x9	Delta 100	90mm	O	N+1	N-1
61.	The Same Pillbox 2006	6x6	Delta 100	80mm	Y/G	N	N
62.	Walberswick Beach 2004	6x9	Delta 100	90mm	O	N+1	N-1
63.	Dunwich Beach 1997	10x8	FP4	300mm	O	N	N
64.	Iken Cliff 1999	6x6	Pan F	80mm	Y/G	N	N
65.	Minsmere from Eastbridge Sluice 2005	6x9	Delta 100	90mm	O	N+1	N-1
66.	Lowestoft Promenade 2003	6x6	Pan F	50mm	Y/G	N	N
67.	Aldeburgh Promenade 2006	6x9	Delta 100	90mm	O	N+1	N-1
68.	Tree near Boyton 2000	6x6	Delta 100	150mm	Y/G	N	N
69.	Bawdsey 2000	6x6	Agfa 100	50mm	Y/G	N+1	N-1
70.	Bawdsey Ferry 2000	6x6	Pan F	50mm	Y/G Grad	N+1	N-1
71.	Snape Church 1999	6x6	Agfa 100	50mm	-	N	N
72.	Felixstowe Docks 2001	6x6	Delta 100	50mm	-	N	N
73.	St James' Green, Southwold 2004	6x9	Delta 100	90mm	O	N+1	N-1
74.	Groynes, Southwold 2003	6x6	Delta 100	50mm	Y/G	N	N
75.	Alde Estuary at Iken Cliff 2004	6x9	Pan F	90mm	O	N+1	N-1
76.	Hurricane Damage, Tunstall Forest 1988	6x6	Pan F	50mm	-	N	N
77.	Turf Farm, Sudbourne 2002	6x6	Delta 100	50mm	Y/G	N	N
78.	Dead Oak Branch, Covehithe 2005	6x6	Delta 100	50mm	Y/G	N	N
79.	Eastbridge Sluice 2009	6x6	Delta 100	50mm	Red	N+1	N-1
80.	Southwold Beach 1997	10x8	HP5	300mm	O	N+1	N-1
81.	Low Tide, Iken Cliff 2009	6x9	Delta 100	90mm	O	N+1	N-1
82.	Fishing Gear, Sizewell 2006	6x9	Delta 100	90mm	O	N+1	N-1
83.	Snow Squall, Aldeburgh 2009	6x6	Delta 100	50mm	Red Grad	N+1	N-1
84.	Ruined Chapel, Eastbridge 2009	6x6	Delta 100	50mm	Red	N+1	N-1
85.	Birches, Thorpeness 2009	6x9	Adox 25	90mm	O	N+1	N-1
86.	Crashing Wave, Aldeburgh 1982	35mm	FP4	28mm	-	N	N
87.	Dunes, Walberswick 2005	6x9	Delta 100	90mm	O	N	N
88.	Ramsholt Church 2002	6x6	Pan F	80mm	Y/G	N+1	N-1
89.	Corporation Marshes 2006	6x6	Agfa 100	50mm	Y/G	N+1	N-1
90.	Boardwalk, Sizewell 1983	35mm	Pan F	28mm	Red	N	N
91.	Shingle Street 2004	6x9	Delta 100	90mm	O	N	N
92.	Surf from Dunwich Cliff 2006	6x9	Delta 100	90mm	O	N+1	N-1
93.	Tidemill, Woodbridge 1999	6x6	Agfa 25	80mm	Y/G	N	N
94.	Pylons, Sizewell 1997	10x8	FP4	165mm	O	N+1	N-1
95.	View Parking, Minsmere 1999	6x6	Agfa 100	80mm	Y/G Grad	N	N
96.	Southwold 2004	6x9	Delta 100	90mm	O	N+1	N-1
97.	Cows at Eastbridge 1998	10x8	HP5	300mm	O	N	N
98.	Thorpeness Beach 2006	6x9	Delta 100	90mm	O	N+1	N-1
99.	Aldeburgh from Thorpeness 2006	6x9	Delta 100	90mm	O	N+1	N-1
100.	Sudbourne Marshes 2007	6x9	Delta 100	90mm	O	N+1	N-1
101.	Snape Maltings 1989	6x6	Agfa 100	50mm	Red	N+1	N-1
102.	Seagulls, Southwold Quay 2005	6x9	Delta 100	90mm	O	N+1	N-1
103.	The River Alde, Slaughden 2004	6x9	Delta 100	90mm	O	N+1	N-1
104.	Thorpe Ness 2007	6x9	Delta 100	90mm	O	N	N
105.	Furthest Point East, Lowestoft 2002	6x6	Agfa 100	50mm	Red	N+1	N-1

Filter: Y/G = Yellow/Green; O= Orange; Grad = Graduated Grey.
Exp: Film exposure; N is correct exposure, N+1 is over exposure.
Dev: Film development; N is normal development, N-1 is under development (-20%), N+1 is over development (+20%).

I do not record shutter speeds and f-stops for roll films (I don't see the point!), I mark the film according to how it was exposed and how it is to be developed.
I do record shutter speeds and f-stops for sheet films as they are developed individually.

Equipment and Materials

Cameras
Canon A-1 with 24mm, 28-55mm, 100-300mm lenses.
Hasselblad 500CM with 50mm, 80mm, and 150mm lenses.
Fuji GS 690 with 90mm lens.
Tachihara 8x10 Field View Camera with Nikon 300mm and 165mm Schneider Kreuznach Super Angulon lenses.

Filters
Yellow/green, orange, red, graduated grey and polarizing by Hoya, Hasselblad, B+W and Cokin.

Tripods
Medium and heavy-weight metal Manfrottos. For the 8x10 I use a large wooden movie tripod.

Exposures
Calculated and films developed according to the Zone System, with the use of a Minolta 5% spot meter.

Film
Ilford FP4 and Pan F in 135 sizes. Ilford FP4, Delta 100, Pan F, XP2, Agfa 100 and 25, Adox 25 in 120 roll film.
Ilford FP4, HP5, Delta 400 in 8x10 sheet film.

Film Developer
Tetenal Ultrafin, Ilford Perceptol, DiXactol by Barry Thornton for roll films. Agfa Rodinal and Kodak HC110 for sheet films.

Printing Paper
Ilford Multigrade Fibre Base Warmtone Glossy. Occasionally I use regular Multigrade, Graded Galerie, Agfa Multicontrast Classic, and Forte Polywarmtone.

Enlarger
Prints are made in a Zone VI cold light enlarger using 80mm, 150mm and 240mm Schneider Componon lenses.

Paper Developer
Ilford Multigrade, Agfa Neutol WA.

Fixing
Ilford Hypam and Rapid Fixer for films and papers. Prints are fixed in two baths and held in the washer until all printing is done. Prints are washed for ten minutes and then treated in Kodak Rapid Selenium Toner and Hypo Clearing Solution or Tetenal Lavaquick. Prints are returned to the washer for thirty minutes, then wiped and laid on plastic mesh screens to dry.

Carl White was born in Cambridge in 1965. Although he started photography at a young age, it was at Bretton Hall College in West Yorkshire where he became increasingly interested in the medium as an art form. Despite graduating in Fine Art he decided that a career in professional photography was the obvious route. He worked in commercial photography until 1993 when he began dividing his time between commercial and personal creative projects. Since 1998 he has been a full-time artist photographer. He lives in France and England where he photographs, exhibits and teaches workshops.

Andrew Hurst was born in 1965. He is a frequent visitor to the Suffolk coast where his personal record for skimming a stone is seven bounces before sinking. He is married with two children and, when not writing, is in practice as a barrister.

Acknowledgments

I would like to acknowledge photographers Jon Gray, Barry Thornton, Fay Godwin and John Nesbitt for their help in ironing out a few technical problems. Many thanks also to author Peter Raby for lots of invaluable help and advice about publishing. To my proofreaders Nicola Jones and Philip White, thank you both very much for your help. Andrew Hurst wishes to acknowledge the following books on which he drew for parts of his Introduction: *The Origins of Suffolk* by Peter Warner and *Dunwich Suffolk* by Jean and Stuart Bacon. He also joins me in thanking Peter Raby for his help.

Finally I would like to thank Andrew for his Introduction. I was thrilled when he agreed to do it!

Old Pond PUBLISHING LTD

In A Long Day
David Kindred and Roger Smith
A rare find of 200 photographs by Ralph and Leonard Titshall of Suffolk farm work and village life from 1925 to 1935. Half the plates show working horses and their horsemen, and there are substantial sections on steam-powered threshing and rural trades. Paperback.

Just a Moment
David Kindred and Roger Smith
The second collection of Titshall photographs compiled by David Kindred. Scenes in Suffolk from the 1920s and '30s show a wide range of farming activities as well as the urban horse, motorised transport, commercial vehicles, men at work and villagers. Paperback

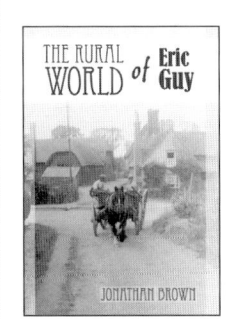

The Rural World of Eric Guy
Jonathan Brown
From the 1930s to the 1960s Eric Guy photographed the rural world around his Berkshire base. Employed freelance by *Farmer & Stockbreeder* and *Farmer's Weekly* he became intimate with the downland farming scene. Jonathan Brown selects 174 of his most striking photographs and provides a knowledgeable text. Paperback

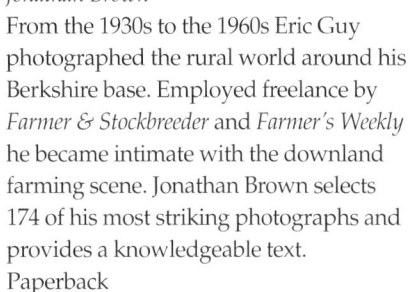

Hadleigh: the portrait of a Suffolk Town
David Kindred
Commercial photographer Peter Boulton recorded the life of this small town in the 1940s and '50s. David Kindred has selected and captioned 200 of Peter Boulton's photographs covering the social and commercial life of Hadleigh in detail. Paperback

Suffolk Steam Railways
David Kindred
From the 1860s to the last days of steam, this collection of photographs deals with the trains, the crews and wider activities of the railways. It shows the main lines, branches and lines now long gone – but not forgotten. Paperback

Farming & Forestry on the Western Front
Murray Maclean
This fine collection of fully captioned photographs from the First World War shows farming activities by the military including early tractors, horse-drawn binders and steam threshing. The second part of the book covers the work of Canadian and other allied foresters in France. Hardback

Free complete catalogue
Old Pond Publishing Ltd, Dencora Business Centre, 36 White House Road, Ipswich IP1 5LT United Kingdom

Website: www.oldpond.com
Phone 01473 238200

Prints of Carl White's photographs can be obtained through his website www.carlwhitephotography.com
Carl White is represented in France by Angle Jaune, l'Atelier Photogalerie, www.anglejaune.fr